The Facts About A Rock Group
Featuring Wings
Introduction by Paul McCartney

By David Gelly
Photographed by Homer Sykes

Series consultant editor: Alan Road

H·A·R·M·O·N·Y B·O·O·K·S

Introduction

Music, like any other business, has come through a lot of changes. When I first started you would plug two guitars and a bass into an amplifier, and with a couple of speakers and microphones, would be off.

Nowadays, something like a big tour requires a much bigger set-up. In this book you can read all about it:– the sound equipment, the lights, the instruments, the people involved, and a host of other things.

Looking through it myself I've found out about things I didn't know went on . . . and so, dear reader, rock and read on!

Paul McCartney

If a typical rock group exists it must be very dull. Wings certainly isn't typical; how could it be, with the legendary figure of Paul McCartney at the helm?

The life of a star group like Wings is constantly changing, particularly when on tour. For example, in Britain concert halls are fairly small and reasonably close together, whereas in the United States they are often enormous and artists have to travel immense distances from one to another. The British tour described here is relaxed and rather cosy by comparison with Wings' subsequent American trip, or their ecstatic visit to Australia. It was only the beginning of a huge and complex undertaking.

Disasters, panics, spectacular scenes and stupendous receptions are bound to occur to a top group as it travels around the world; these are the moments you read about in the press. In this book we have set out to give the rest of the picture, the everyday routine which even the most eminent must follow. To get their music to the people they have to tour, record, employ specialists with particular skills and talents. This is the process which we describe here in words and pictures.

Dave Gelly
Homer Sykes

Wings

Paul McCartney

Paul McCartney has his name on more hit songs than any modern rock writer, first in collaboration with John Lennon and now on his own or together with his wife, Linda. As a Beatle he was part of the greatest phenomenon in popular music history, and continues to be the finest inventor of rock melodies. His father was a pianist and dance-band leader in his youth and trained Paul's naturally acute musical ear from early childhood.

With the break-up of the Beatles in 1970 McCartney produced his first solo record, on which he played and sang all the parts. 'Ram' followed; then he formed Wings, recording the albums 'Wildlife', 'Red Rose Speedway', 'Band On The Run' and 'Venus And Mars', as well as many hit singles.

A curious mixture of the quiet, retiring man and the natural stage performer, he continues to command a huge and devoted following—from teenagers who don't remember the Beatles to their parents and even grandparents. McCartney is a fine pianist and guitarist, but his main instrument is the bass guitar, of which he is one of the world's finest exponents. His voice is immensely flexible and warm and is perfectly attuned to his songwriting style.

He lives with Linda and children Heather, Mary and Stella in St. John's Wood, London, and at their farm near Campbelltown in Scotland.

Linda McCartney

A successful rock photographer before her marriage to Paul in 1969, Linda has become an inseparable part of the Wings sound with her keyboard playing. Although she had always loved music, she never played before meeting Paul. Despite this, she has considerable musical flair and takes the job extremely seriously.

Linda confesses herself to be in awe of her husband's talent. "I just don't know how he does it," she says about his apparent ability to pluck perfect tunes out of thin air.

She has very firm views about what constitutes a sane life for her family and refuses to allow the frantic pace of the rock world to disturb the upbringing of the McCartney children. Both Linda and Paul go to great lengths to maintain the 'family' atmosphere of the whole Wings idea, insisting on being involved with every aspect of the work and knowing everyone personally. She is forceful and uncompromising in such matters, but also gentle and very kind to fans and crew alike.

Denny Laine

The friendship between Denny Laine and Paul McCartney is a long-standing one based on mutual admiration. McCartney has held a high opinion of Denny's work ever since he was a member of the Moody Blues. It was with the Moodies that Laine recorded his great hit, 'Go Now', a number which is an inevitable feature of Wings' stage act.

Along with Paul and Linda, he forms the core of the band's music; indeed the most successful Wings album to date, 'Band On The Run', was made by just the three of them singing and playing all the parts.

"I think I've got some idea of the way he feels about things," says Denny of McCartney. "I know the kind of pressure he's under because I've been through a lot of the same stuff myself. The longer you go on the tougher it is in lots of ways. People expect more and more of you. For Paul, having been part of the best rock 'n' roll band in history, it must be very heavy. I admire him so much, the way he handles it and doesn't let it interfere with his music."

Jimmy McCulloch

A child prodigy and working musician from the age of thirteen, Jimmy McCulloch is a diminutive Glaswegian with an impressive track-record. He first came to notice on Thunderclap Newman's Number 1 hit, 'Something In The Air', and subsequently played with John Mayall and Stone The Crows. His composition 'Medicine Jar' is featured on 'Venus And Mars' and in Wings' stage-show.

McCulloch is a virtuoso guitarist whose solos with Wings are one of the band's most potent ingredients.

Joe English

Despite his name, Joe English is an American from Rochester, New York. Tony Dorsey, the arranger and trombonist, spoke so highly of his drumming that McCartney asked Joe to attend the recordings of 'Venus And Mars' in 1975. Shortly afterwards, he was invited to join Wings. A Beatle-fan from his teenage years, English jumped at the chance.

A master of many drumming styles and a first-rate technician on his instrument, English brings a fire and impetus to the band which his predecessors could never quite manage. Tireless, cheerful, enthusiastic and a perfectionist in all things, he shares the McCartneys' love of farming and country life as well. It is difficult to imagine a more perfect man for the job.

Roadies

Wings' home and operational base is at EMI's film studios just north of London. They occupy a gigantic but curiously temporary-looking structure, rather like an aircraft hangar, known as a sound-stage. The building is surrounded by a wilderness of weeds and coarse grass, out of which pokes a surrealistic collection of objects—two flights of ornamental stairs, half a Spitfire, and a village street with a German U-Boat parked at the end of it.

Inside, McCartney rehearses the band, amplification is tested and retested, lights are rigged and experts of all kinds come and go, discussing their various specialities with casual efficiency. In one corner is a work-bench, around which the band's permanent four-man crew work busily.

In charge of the crew is road-manager Trevor Jones. All the practicalities of the forthcoming tour center on him; he carries a thousand details in his head as he sets out the stage, settles arguments, arranges the day's activities, orders spares. He never looks harassed, but confesses that sometimes he wakes up in a cold sweat, worrying about some vital piece of planning which isn't working out.

"I go home at night and sit thinking about the day, cross off six items from the top of the list and add another dozen at the bottom. You work day-to-day, but there's always something that hangs on as a potential source of trouble."

In an operation as big as this there has to be somebody to carry the can, to turn the vast plan into working reality. Trevor is one of life's

copers; he has the qualities of an army general. Napoleon could have used him.

The other three Wings crewmen look after specific instruments. John Hammel is the guitar expert, Ted Sellen takes care of the drums, and Rocky Morley seems to know everything there is to know about keyboard instruments.

The term 'roadie', which is generally applied to men like these, doesn't really do them justice. Their knowledge and ability to solve technical problems quickly and without fuss deserves a dignified title—not that they bother much about titles.

Since there is no career-structure in the music business, roadies arrive in their jobs by a variety of routes. Many are ex-musicians themselves, like Rocky Morley. He started as a guitarist.

"I wasn't a good enough player—at least I didn't think I was—to stick at playing in bands. And I was getting more and more interested in organs and their working parts, so when I was asked I started doing this job." Whatever he may have thought of his own talents as a guitarist,

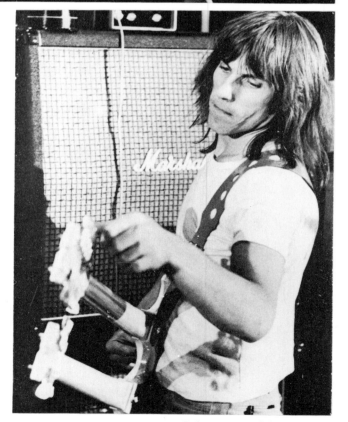

Guitar expert John Hammel

5

he's worked for some pretty good bands in his time, including Amen Corner, Vanilla Fudge and Bonzo Dog.

Before joining Wings for the British tour, Rocky had been with Keith Emerson of ELP, a man renowned for doing grievous bodily harm to electronic keyboards. Linda McCartney treats instruments with much more respect, of course, but the rigors of touring mean that they get shaken up and sometimes damaged.

"The manufacturers design organs for people to take home and polish and play in their living rooms. They're not made to be bumped around or constantly taken to pieces and re-assembled," says Rocky.

He takes care of:

A C3 Hammond Organ
A Mellotron
A Hohner Clavinet
An ARP Synthesizer
A Mini-Moog Synthesizer
A Fender-Rhodes Electric Piano.

The Mellotron is particularly complicated. It can reproduce the sound of any instrument by activating strips of pre-recorded tape. A tape can jam or get out of line and untangling it is a tricky business. The essence of Rocky's job is to pinpoint a fault quickly, which means having a complete and instinctive grasp of the electrical and mechanical works of each instrument.

For John Hammel the main concern must be the sheer *number* of instruments he has to deal with. According to their insurance list, Wings have 37 guitars—electric, acoustic, bass, pedal steel, twin-neck, custom-built and production models. Matters are further complicated by the fact that McCartney plays left-handed, so there are left and right-hand versions of most instruments. Of course, not all the guitars go on tour; some are kept permanently at home by their owners. But at the end of each day there's a row of cases a couple of yards long for John Hammel to check over. It's a good thing he's a guitar lover and collector in his own right.

For Ted Sellen things are a bit easier, with two kits (Gretsch and Camco) and various accessories, together with four Nigerian congas and a pile of tambourines, maracas, sticks, pedals and

spares. Because he isn't in specific charge of electronic equipment, Ted is kept pretty busy doing general stage work and helping out the others.

Sound

Fans come to rock concerts expecting to hear the music they already know from a group's records. It sounds like a simple requirement, but fulfilling it is a very complicated and expensive undertaking. As we shall see later, recording is a long, subtle process and reproducing the same effect in a big hall takes a lot of thought and expertise.

The heart of a live performance is the public address (P.A.) system. Anyone who has attended one of these shows will have noticed the huge bank of loudspeakers on each side of the stage, a giant assemblage of black boxes reaching from the stage almost to the roof. These are the business end of an electronic chain, starting with the guitar strings and vocal chords of the performers, and passing through amplifiers, mixers and yet more amplifiers to the P.A., which carries the sound into the auditorium.

At the start of rehearsals for the tour McCartney, in typically thoroughgoing manner, sat down and considered the P.A. system he would need. Having drawn up a general specification, in consultation with Trevor Jones and manager Brian Brolly, he asked various firms to submit equipment for the group to try out. Many leading British companies, with long experience of big-time rock tours, designed systems and brought them along. Each Wings rehearsal became a testing session for a new idea, but there was always the same problem: the band weren't comfortable because they couldn't tell what they sounded like from the front.

Every P.A. system includes 'monitor' speakers which feed the sound to the musicians on stage, but Wings were unhappy about this part of all the schemes they tried. In the end they decided to look abroad, and Showco of Dallas, Texas, came up with the perfect design for the job. Not only did Showco draw up the scheme, they provided the equipment and sent their own three-man team to operate it. That is how Jack

6

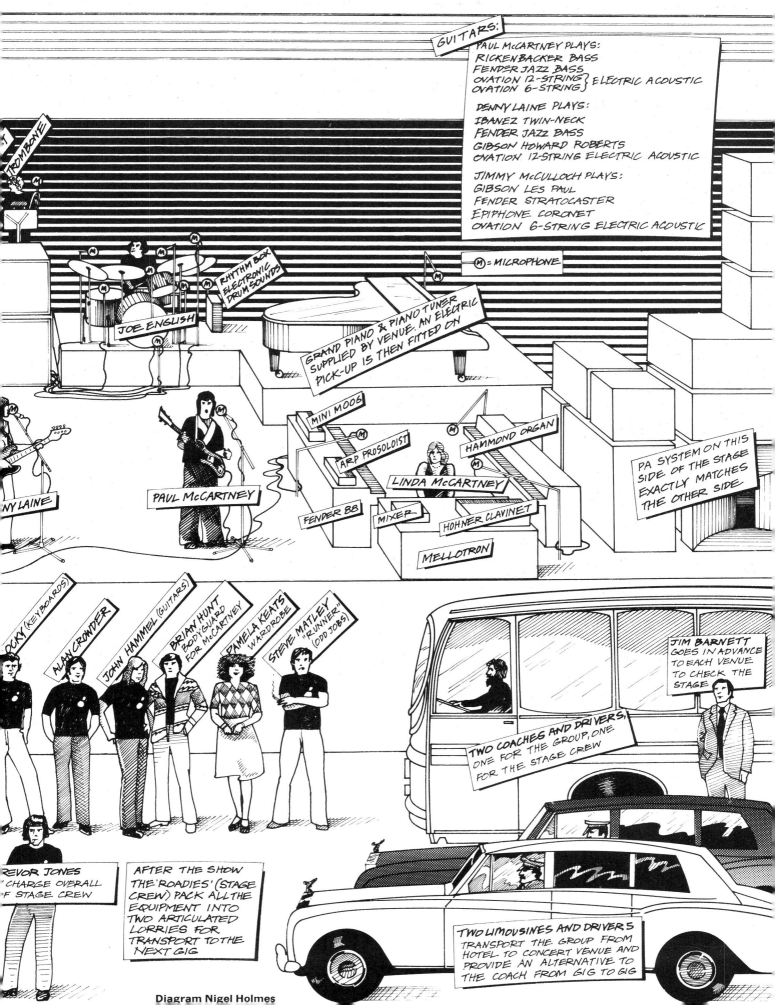

GUITARS:

PAUL McCARTNEY PLAYS:
RICKENBACKER BASS
FENDER JAZZ BASS
OVATION 12-STRING
OVATION 6-STRING } ELECTRIC ACOUSTIC

DENNY LAINE PLAYS:
IBANEZ TWIN-NECK
FENDER JAZZ BASS
GIBSON HOWARD ROBERTS
OVATION 12-STRING ELECTRIC ACOUSTIC

JIMMY McCULLOCH PLAYS:
GIBSON LES PAUL
FENDER STRATOCASTER
EPIPHONE CORONET
OVATION 6-STRING ELECTRIC ACOUSTIC

TROMBONE

M = MICROPHONE

RHYTHM BOX ELECTRONIC DRUM SOUNDS

JOE ENGLISH

GRAND PIANO & PIANO TUNER SUPPLIED BY VENUE. AN ELECTRIC PICK-UP IS THEN FITTED ON

MINI MOOG

ARP PROSOLOIST

HAMMOND ORGAN

PA SYSTEM ON THIS SIDE OF THE STAGE EXACTLY MATCHES THE OTHER SIDE

PAUL McCARTNEY

LINDA McCARTNEY

FENDER 88

MIXER

HOHNER CLAVINET

MELLOTRON

NY LAINE

[OCKY] (KEYBOARDS)

ALAN CROWDER

JOHN HAMMEL (GUITARS)

BRIAN HUNT BODYGUARD FOR McCARTNEY

PAMELA KEATS WARDROBE

STEVE MATLEY "RUNNER" (ODD JOBS)

JIM BARNETT GOES IN ADVANCE TO EACH VENUE TO CHECK THE STAGE

TWO COACHES AND DRIVERS, ONE FOR THE GROUP, ONE FOR THE STAGE CREW

REVOR JONES CHARGE OVERALL F STAGE CREW

AFTER THE SHOW THE 'ROADIES' (STAGE CREW) PACK ALL THE EQUIPMENT INTO TWO ARTICULATED LORRIES FOR TRANSPORT TO THE NEXT GIG

TWO LIMOUSINES AND DRIVERS TRANSPORT THE GROUP FROM HOTEL TO CONCERT VENUE AND PROVIDE AN ALTERNATIVE TO THE COACH FROM GIG TO GIG

Diagram Nigel Holmes

Maxson, Morris Lyda and Craig Schertz came to join the Wings touring party.

The basis of Showco's system lies in the monitors. These are set and balanced first, so that everyone on stage can hear exactly the sound that the band is producing. Only after this is done is the sound fed to the P.A. speakers in front. The arrangement requires two sets of control gear, one for the monitors (operated by Morris Lyda) and one for the P.A. (Jack Maxson), with Craig Schertz acting as assistant to both.

Rehearsing

Rehearsals proceed with strict regularity, five days a week. Each one is scheduled to last four hours with a break half-way through, although they often don't bother to stop once they've got started.

McCartney concentrates on the music as much as possible, leaving the crew to take care of other matters, and he sets a pretty fierce pace compared with many star leaders. He is gifted with a superb musical ear which catches the slightest fault in intonation or timing, and he refuses to let anything go until he is entirely satisfied. He stops the band in mid-flight:

"No, it's too fuzzy. The harmonies aren't sharp enough." Going over to the piano, he starts sorting out everybody's notes. Like a choirmaster, he takes each part separately, changing the voicing here and there until it all meshes smoothly.

"We've really got to concentrate all the time here, otherwise it'll go limp. And don't *scoop* up to that last note; let it fall away naturally."

In the end he's spent twenty-five minutes on five notes, but the result is clear and tight—a beautiful, airy sound.

But there are dangers in rehearsal too.

"You can over-rehearse, get fed up with the numbers and fed up with each other," says McCartney. "We got to a point at one time when we were very gloomy, moaning that it wasn't jelling. And that made it worse, of course.

Trombone player Tony Dorsey

So in the end we had a discussion-cum-argument about the whole thing and everybody got it out of their system. We decided that each of us would play his own bit instead of looking over his shoulder at the next man. And it seemed to work."

As luck would have it, this piece of group-therapy coincided with the arrival of Tony Dorsey and the horn section. Their energy and high spirits acted as a tonic. At the end of the day the rehearsal turned into a riotous jam-session, with everyone playing someone else's instrument (Wings are all amazingly multi-talented) and McCartney even blowing a passable trumpet solo.

"That's when we started believing in it. It became *real* for us that day, and everybody felt much happier."

As the tour date approaches, detailed rehearsal gives way to complete runs of the show. As it knits together one can see what McCartney means by 'realness'. It begins to feel like a show rather than a rehearsal.

The full P.A. system has now been installed and the lighting men are working on their own arrangements. By this stage Wings really need their enormous building, not only to fit everything together, but because space means resonance, and the speakers are built to resound in a large auditorium.

A whole new crop of problems comes with the introduction of the lights. At one point, for instance, the speakers set up a terrifying hum every time the stage floodlights are turned on.

The sound stage rings with Texan curses as the Showco men descend on the offending equipment.

There is just one big hurdle to jump before the tour starts, a concert to an invited audience at the rehearsal studio.

"It was a tough audience," McCartney says. "Record company people and so forth, and it showed up a lot of holes in the show—bits that needed to be tightened up."

The sound stage was packed to the roof, and the applause sounded heartfelt enough, but McCartney detected points where it wasn't as strong as it might have been and made some last-minute alteration to the program. There was nothing left for him to do now except wait for the first show of the tour: the Gaumont, Southampton.

On Tour

Packing an articulated truck goes on the same principle as packing a suitcase. Everything has its place—the heaviest stuff at the bottom—and it must be packed tight, with no room to shift or rattle about during the journey.

On the first attempt there is much trial and error. The crew roll the heavy cabinets and trunks up the loading ramp, often having to take a run at it to get enough impetus, and sometimes have to roll them down and start again. It's a long, tedious job in which everyone takes part. Although Trevor Jones is in charge, he never has to give specific orders. He makes suggestions, keeps stock of what is still waiting, and heaves and shoves with the rest.

The men from Showco go at it in typically Texan fashion, whooping and yelling and bawling acid comments on each other's performance. Although they take the job seriously, there is the occasional comic outburst. "Me Drongo!"

calls a caveman voice from the back of a trailer. "Drongo strong! Drongo lift trunk! Drongo break leg . . . Arrgh!"

By the time the tail-gates are closed and locked, every piece of gear has been found a place; the place it will occupy between shows for the next couple of weeks. There is only one casualty after the first trip; Howie Casey's tenor saxophone, which has been bumped a bit too hard and, despite a stout case, has had one of its delicate key-rods bent. Fortunately he has been able to get a temporary replacement while it is being fixed.

At each new hall the crew will have to unload $12\frac{1}{2}$ tons and load it up again afterwards. In between they will be doing their own specialized and highly technical jobs. They don't finish until around 1:00 A.M., and have to be ready to leave at 8:00 the same morning. It's unbelievably tiring, particularly when you consider the irregular and often rather sketchy meals that Steve Huntley, the crew's runner, has to rustle up for them. Trevor Jones has an

elaborate array of vitamin tablets to supplement this diet, and says that he would find the work impossible without them.

There is also the matter of shoes. The endless humping, walking and simply standing still is very hard on the feet. All the crew wear flat, comfortable shoes with springy soles. Except, that is, for the Texans, who retain the high-heeled Western boots that they are used to.

Even before Wings had put the finishing touches to their program, the first of the complex, interlocking tour movements had begun. Jim Barnett, the Advance Rigger, was in Southampton, checking that the Gaumont stage was ready to receive $12\frac{1}{2}$ tons of P.A. gear, monitors, lights, backdrops and control-boards. By the time it all turns up he will have moved on to Bristol, Cardiff, Manchester. Once the show arrives everything must be ready to roll smoothly into place.

At 8:00 A.M. the crew assemble on the steps of London's Hammersmith Odeon, the scene of two forthcoming shows, to board the bus for the first leg of the journey. Most of them drift off to a nearby workmen's café for tea and bacon sandwiches, as Trevor checks his lists and looks out for the coach, which is already 15 minutes late. When it finally arrives everyone troops aboard. Morris Lyda stretches full-length on the rear seat and falls fast asleep immediately —a knack acquired from long experience of irregular hours on the road. A film crew clamber on as well, focussing on dozy morning faces as

the bus grinds through early rush-hour traffic.

Jack Maxson, Showco's P.A. expert, has brought an elaborate cassette-player along and sits immobile as a wooden Indian, his head encased in a pair of enormous Koss headphones, for the entire journey. The rest have to make do with Radio One on the coach loudspeaker.

It's raining at 10:30 A.M. in Southampton and already there's a hitch; a truck hasn't arrived. One of the massive Volvo 88s is backed up to the loading bay, but the other's nowhere to be seen. The crew set to work with what they've got. Within minutes Ted Sellen is hammering nails into the piano rostrum to keep the instrument steady, while the rest work out the placing of key pieces of equipment. In the cab of the truck Mick, the driver, sits smoking as he awaits the arrival of his partner.

Mick used to be a roadie himself, working with the Rolling Stones and Billy Preston, but he prefers to drive the 'artic'. So long as he gets the gear to the theatre on time he can arrange his own schedule. His is a night-shift job essentially, and the routine suits him. He is enthusiastic about the Volvo which handles, he claims, like a Mini. What happens if he gets its huge bulk stuck on a tight corner?

"I don't get it stuck," he says laconically.

The cab is fitted with stereo tape and radio and a narrow bed behind the seats. This is for use when there are two drivers working in relays on long runs. With the short journeys of a British tour Mick stays in a hotel like the rest of the crew, sleeping in the daytime.

The second truck finally arrives at 11:30 and rigging can go ahead unhindered. Jack Maxson's enormous P.A. control board and accessory rack is to go at the back of the auditorium. Some theatres now have specially prepared places for P.A. control, since all touring rock shows need the facility. However, the Gaumont has not yet had this done, so Jack supervises a couple of local workmen as they build an alarmingly rickety-looking structure across the backs of some stalls seats. A great, serpentine skein of taped-together cables stretches out across the hall, dangling from ornamental cornices and the underside of the circle. It connects Jack's board with Morris' monitor control at the side of the stage.

Jack is not happy with the arrangement, not so much because of the improvised housing for his equipment, but because of its position. Immediately behind his back-row seat is the rear gangway bearing the notice, '42 Persons Standing', and the last thing he wants is 'persons' hanging about where they can distract him during the show. He needs all his concentration to listen and balance, and to follow the plan, which is written on cards—one for each number.

Despite all hitches and setbacks, the road-crew have an inflexible deadline when all rigging must be completed: the 5:00 P.M. sound-check. This is when McCartney and the band arrive to run through part of the show, to test the gear and adjust it to the acoustics of the hall. At

every hall they need to go through this process, and every time there's something that needs seeing-to.

Before they even start, Linda McCartney discovers that one of the synthesizers has put itself out of tune. This sometimes happens, spontaneously and for no apparent reason. Rocky and Trevor set upon it and coax it back into line, and Wings strike up with 'Venus And Mars'. They don't coast through the sound-check; they play and sing at full pressure to give as complete a picture as possible to Morris and Jack, and to judge the hall for themselves. If the check is long and troublesome this can take as long as the show itself, and be as tiring.

Meanwhile, manager Brian Brolly is prowling around the auditorium, inspecting the sight-lines, making sure that everyone is visible from everywhere and that the lighting effects are as

The Horn Section

14

good at the back of the circle as in the front stalls. He discovers that the back-drops are only half-visible from the back. They are lowered and promptly disappear behind a bank of P.A. The crew juggle them into some kind of compromise and Brolly makes a note to sort the problem out for future shows.

Horn Section

Wings are augmented on tour by four wind-instrumentalists, known for convenience as the 'horn section'. While sophisticated gadgets like the Mellotron can reproduce a lot of recorded effects, there is no substitute for the live sound of real instruments. The horn section consists of three Americans and one Englishman. They are:

Steve 'Tex' Howard—trumpet & flugelhorn
Thaddeus Richard—soprano & alto saxophones, clarinet & flute
Howie Casey—tenor saxophone
Tony Dorsey—trombone.

Apart from playing trombone, Tony Dorsey also writes the arrangements for the section and leads it. He exudes musicianship and good humor in equal proportions from every pore of his gigantic frame. Tony used to be Musical Director for soul-singer Joe Tex and first worked with McCartney on the recording of 'Venus And Mars' in New Orleans.

Thaddeus and Steve were his choices for the tour, and they play beautifully throughout. It is very difficult to produce a good performance in short bursts as they have to, a few chords here and a brief solo there. Instruments are apt to go out of tune and the balance between each man has to be struck perfectly, at once and without preparation.

Howie Casey, a fellow Liverpudlian, has been a friend of McCartney's since beat pre-history, 15 years ago. They both worked impossibly hard (six hours a night, seven nights a week) at the famous—or infamous—Star Club in Hamburg. Howie's solo on the recording of 'Bluebird' is a vital part of a classic song. Nevertheless, he had forgotten it and had to re-learn his own music from the record especially for the tour. Of course, he could have made up another solo just as good—a different one every night even—but the aim is to reproduce the recorded version as perfectly as possible.

Several bands carry semi-permanent horn sections. The Kinks, for example, invariably augment their live sound in this way. Others add even larger groups of players, although this can cause difficulties if they encounter small stages in their travels. Alan Price could hardly squeeze himself in front of a phalanx of strings and brass on at least one occasion.

Scenery

McCartney has always been renowned for his 'style'. Although no one ever seems able to define this quality exactly, it comes out in his care about the whole appearance of Wings on stage.

To put his ideas into practice, and to contribute more, he engaged stage-designer Ian Knight, a specialist in devising settings for rock shows. Although he uses the same means as theatrical designers—lights, scenery, special effects—Ian Knight's job is surrounded by special limitations and difficulties which would drive his colleagues in the theater to distraction.

"There is a basic difference between designing for the theater and designing for a rock show. In rock you have to start with the music—the band and all its equipment. They've rehearsed in a certain way, standing or sitting where they feel comfortable. Now, if you intrude on this and start moving them about for visual effect you could ruin the whole thing. I've found this not only with Wings, but also with The Who and Led Zeppelin. You *mustn't* disturb the natural setting of the band. Their music comes from playing together, from feeling each other's presence; communicating without speaking or even looking at each other. It's a delicate balance and must be left alone. A rock designer's first job is to let the music breathe."

By contrast, the theater is a much simpler proposition. "You have a director. He devises the whole thing and the actors fit into the scheme as it evolves. I can't think of many rock groups who would accept this kind of direction. You may see television shows like Midnight Special which seem to be organized this way, but the groups are only miming, so it doesn't matter how they're set up. Only certain types of show can take total direction, like the Osmonds for instance. They have a Las Vegas choreographer to build up their act. And Bowie and Alice Cooper put on highly produced shows, but they're one-man affairs with the band out of the picture to all intents and purposes."

Ian Knight's plan for Wings includes a pair of enormous lighting gantries carrying batteries of colored floodlights, together with a complicated network of 'spots' mounted around the hall. The whole thing is controlled from a board, not unlike the P.A. equipment at first glance. It is another Showco speciality and is operated by Kirby Wyatt and Alan Owen. Not only do they have to operate the vast array of controls in front of them, following Ian Knight's plan, they also have to give orders through a microphone to the men working spotlights away up in the balcony.

Some songs are illustrated by pictures painted on backdrops and lowered behind the band. 'C Moon', for instance, has a copy of a work by the surrealist painter, René Magritte; a candle with the moon sitting on top, where the flame ought to be. McCartney has the original painting at home. David Hockney's painting 'Chair' goes with the song.

The crew have a lot of trouble with these drops because it's hard to judge exactly the correct height for them. Each night the stage is a slightly different shape, so there has to be a lot of trial and error.

Wardrobe

Costume designer Celia Baker

Solo artists like Elton John often wear extravagant, even outlandish, costumes, but few groups go in for special outfits. This may well be a reaction to the uniformed formality of early rock 'n' roll days, but even the biggest names tend to cultivate a kind of studied scruffiness.

Wings' stage clothes are not exactly fancy dress, but neither are they jeans and tee-shirt. They were designed and made by Celia Baker and Tony Walker; their only instruction from the McCartneys was to think of something interesting in the colors of the 'Venus And Mars' album jacket (red, yellow, black and white).

They drew up some design ideas and took them, together with fabric-samples, to the band for approval. Celia and Tony only had three weeks to do the whole job, from design to delivery, but they managed it. Most of the pitfalls were avoided; for instance, long skirts for Linda (get caught in the undercarriage of keyboard instruments), heavy materials (unbearable under hot lights), or long, loose sleeves (impossible for drummers).

A few problems did surface when the clothes were first tried out. Jimmy McCulloch had a beautiful satin jacket, but it didn't have any pockets. Guitar players have to have somewhere to put plectrums and other bits and pieces, so pockets were added. It turned out also that red clothes under various coloured lights, although they are very effective on stage, look distinctly odd on color television. The camera gives them a strange, muddy appearance. So *that* had to be changed.

But the effect when the lights come up for the first number, all the band in their different colors and the stage in half-shadow, is wonderfully mysterious.

"It's not the most glamorous job in the show," says Pamela Keats. She looks after the wardrobe —principally the band's stage clothes, but also the special tee-shirts worn by the road crew.

Wardrobe lady Pamela Keats with Linda McCartney

As soon as the crew bus arrives at a new hall, Pamela bags a dressing-room near the stage and sets up her ironing-board and hanger-rails and starts unpacking trunks. Then she goes in search of a laundromat. "You don't know what trouble is," she says, "until you've tried getting something cleaned in 2 hours at a 2-hour cleaners."

As soon as Wings come off stage they change out of their gear and give it to Pamela. It's not made for sitting about in and, anyway, each garment has to be checked for damage or wear before it is packed. On the following day, while the crew are setting up and the band is checking the sound, Pamela will be repairing and ironing.

After a few days, a duplicate set of costumes arrives from Celia Baker, which takes some of the urgency out of this process, but it's still a race against time and the 2-hour cleaners.

Wings fans from America

Fans

At about lunchtime the first fans begin to gather outside the theatre. Among the earliest are Mr. & Mrs. Charles D. Cobb of Greenville, Kentucky. They have hitch-hiked from London on the off-chance of getting a ticket.

"We saw in the paper that Wings were going to play—then we turned the page and read that all the shows were sold out. But where there's a will there's a way. So far we've managed to get just one ticket off a guy who came with one spare; I guess we'll get another by the time the show starts. We haven't come all this way to give up without a real good try."

* * * * * *

There are eight American fans, together with several from Germany, Scandinavia and one Japanese girl, who have come over to Britain specifically to follow this tour. They travel independently, of course, staying in bed-and-breakfast accommodation and making use of British Rail holiday passes to get from town to town. One of the American girls estimated that the complete cost of the trip, including air-fare, concert tickets and living expenses, came to about $1800 each.

A curious kind of arms-length comradeship grows up between them and the touring party. Each morning they emerge from their guest-houses and gather outside the group's hotel to see them leave.

"Hello, still here then?" calls McCartney cheerfully, as he comes through the swing doors with Linda and the children. He stops for a brief chat; they take each other's picture as he stands with them and wave as the bus pulls away.

By this time the little gathering has grown into quite a crowd, with passers-by, local office-workers and shop assistants joining in. It melts away quickly as the local people get on with the day's work and the faithful followers hurry off to the station.

Security

In and around the theatre the day moves to a steadily accelerating tempo. As the crew get on with rigging, and the first fans begin to roost along the front steps, Mr. D. O. McCoy, the Assistant Manager, gets down to details with Steve Matley, the promoter's representative. In a few hours the building will be virtually under siege, so security, safety and timing must all be perfect. As well as this, supplies of backstage food and drink must be arranged, displays and posters checked, and staff briefed. Mr. McCoy will be responsible this evening for 2250 people's safety and comfort; he cannot leave anything to chance.

The number of big theaters is declining every year as more and more cinemas are converted to multi-screen complexes. This means that places like Southampton Gaumont or Cardiff Capitol are in great demand for one-night shows.

Different acts attract different types of audience, and they need looking after in different ways. When Diana Ross appears people dress up for the occasion; the atmosphere is enthusiastic but sober. On such nights only normal theatre security is needed and the bars are open during the interval. By contrast, a heavy band like Status Quo gets a much more boisterous reception. Additional security men are brought in and all the bars stay firmly closed, to prevent enthusiasm turning to riot.

Very young audiences need special care. Being small and determined, they can wriggle under and through the best defenses and, should anything go wrong, the press is always eager for someone to blame—as several theater managers have had cause to remember after concerts by the Osmonds or the Bay City Rollers.

But Wings' followers are, on the whole, an amiable, orderly crowd. So long as there isn't a bomb-scare (his biggest nightmare), Mr. McCoy looks forward to a happy, trouble-free night.

Before, during and after a concert there is only one way into a theater—through the front door with a ticket. But not everybody accepts this simple arrangement, so a lot of effort has to go into enforcing security.

Every building has weak spots. Windows, doors, fire-escapes, loading-bays, any place that is not actually a brick wall can be made to admit an intruder. At one Wings concert a would-be concert-goer was spotted hanging from a drainpipe three stories above the ground. He had got *up*, but couldn't get *in*.

In most cases the theater's own staff can watch the obvious points, while the local police are usually on hand as well. But there is one place which always gives trouble: the stage door. Since it is the only opening, apart from the front entrance, this inconspicuous little alleyway always attracts a crowd. They come knowing that the stars *must* pass through here and their air of expectancy and excitement draws others. Most are content to wait, calling, waving and generally enjoying the event. But there are always potential gatecrashers and these have to be kept out.

If only the artists and crew were allowed in there would be no problem, but in an operation as complex as this there are dozens of authorized people—publicists, record company executives, promoters' staff, invited guests. To make sure that they are admitted, each is provided with a collection of items to wear that amounts almost to a complete uniform. Each person travelling with the band has a black tee-shirt with the 'Venus And Mars' emblem, a badge bearing the Wings symbol and his name, and a large square sticker called a 'stage pass' which he attaches to himself in some prominent position. Thus equipped, one can pass through the stage door as through the air-lock in a space capsule.

The number of people backstage is a constant headache to Trevor Jones. He has enough problems as it is and bodies cluttering up his work area can seriously hamper him.

"It's alright if they stay in the dressing-rooms and corridors," he says, "but when they hang about at the edge of the stage they are in the way. Not only that, there are ropes and cables all over the place that they can fall over, and a lot of the cables carry power. One day someone will get hurt."

London concerts are notorious for the numbers who try to get in backstage. The entertainment industry is concentrated there—recording, journalism, management—and a lot of people claim entry because of their business connection. The stage door staff have to be tough if they are to prevent the crew getting swamped, but diplomatic at the same time.

Another aspect of security, and one of growing importance, is the matter of unauthorized recording. The development of miniature transistorised cassette recorders has made it possible for anyone to sit in a theatre and take down the proceedings on a machine weighing only a few pounds. The result won't be exactly hi-fi but, with luck, it will be quite acceptable. Now *any* unofficial recording is a form of stealing, because it takes someone's work without permission and without paying for it. In the case of the average fan it's only a technical crime, but often the cassette will be copied and sold, even, on occasion, produced as a record, complete with illustrated sleeve. This is called 'bootlegging' and it infuriates everyone concerned—the band, the songwriter, the music publisher and the record company.

As well as stealing an artist's work, the bootlegger can also damage his reputation by issuing a record which is below the usual high standard. That's the thing which annoys McCartney most.

"I paid $6.40 for a cassette called 'McCartney At Hammersmith'," says manager Brian Brolly. "It was so bad you just couldn't tell what *song* was being performed half the time!"

Apart from being dishonest, bootlegging a McCartney show is a waste of time, because everything played by Wings on stage has already been definitively recorded.

Scalpers

If the concert you want to go to is sold-out, there are two things you can do; either get there early and hang about to see if anyone turns up with a spare ticket, or patronize one of the professional gentlemen known unflatteringly as 'scalpers'. You will see them outside all big events—football matches, fights, West End theaters, opera and ballet, as well as rock shows.

Nothing will induce a scalper to reveal his source of supply, although it is not necessarily an illegal one. He simply has some system of getting to the head of the advance-booking line, and that system is his closely-guarded secret.

The vast majority of tickets bought from scalpers are perfectly alright, but occasionally there will be a rash of forgeries. This usually happens when the face value of the tickets is especially high. The official price of a seat to one of Sinatra's concerts can be in the $30.00—$70.00 bracket, and the black-market figure could go several times higher. The temptation to make a few hundred dollars extra by printing phony tickets proves irresistible in such cases.

Rock fans can't afford Sinatra-type prices, though, and black-market tickets don't often go for more than $15.00 in the provinces and $75.00 in London. One of the scalpers at McCartney's Bristol concert claimed, however, to have sold a Rolling Stones ticket for $470.00.

When challenged about their actions, scalpers will advance a defense of the profit-motive which would do credit to the Chamber of Commerce At the same time, they will claim that their other goods—badges, posters, programs and so forth—are actually *cheaper* than the official items on sale inside the theater; although this doesn't apply to Wings concerts because McCartney Productions don't go in for fringe-sales. They only sell programs and, unlike many rock programs, these are good value for money—well produced and packed with pictures and information.

In Concert

The first concert goes well, much to everyone's relief. Despite the meticulous rehearsal and that private show a few days previously, there is no way of being sure it's all going to work. But as the first strains of 'Venus And Mars' rise from the darkened stage, a solid wall of cheering comes back from the crowd. It is a warm, affectionate sound; not hysterical, but full of delight and pleasurable anticipation.

McCartney has taken great pains over the program. Most of the songs come from the two most recent albums, 'Band On The Run' and 'Venus And Mars'; but he has delved back to the Beatle days for old favorites like 'Yesterday' and 'Lady Madonna', and also includes the very complex theme song that he wrote for the

James Bond film, 'Live And Let Die'. It's one thing to build up a piece like this over several days in a recording studio, but another matter altogether to reproduce the effect faultlessly, in one go, in front of 2500 people. You can see why he goes to such lengths over detail at rehearsals.

There are, of course, the inevitable hitches. At one point McCartney's guitar amplification cuts out. It is discovered that this is simply because a jack-plug has come out of its socket on the instrument. He has taken the usual precaution of looping the cable around the neck-strap, but in the excitement has stepped on it and pulled it loose. John Hammel creeps on stage and replaces the plug.

When the show is over and Wings have

played two encores to a standing ovation, everyone comes backstage, laughing euphorically.

"I've never felt so relaxed," says McCartney. "Never mind the problems, it was a good show, right, Denny?" Denny Laine grins and nods.

"It's been like climbing a long, steep hill, and now we're coasting down the other side," McCartney reflects.

"I don't like counting chickens before they're hatched, but it's a good omen for the rest of the tour."

His instinct is proved right over the next couple of weeks. In every town audiences are ecstatic, particularly in Liverpool, his home town and the birthplace of the Beatles. The whole band now has an ease and confidence which communicates itself to the fans and turns the tour into a triumphal progress.

Thoughtful fans, sitting in the auditorium during a rock concert, often wonder how much profit the band is making for its evening's work. The answer is likely to be 'none at all', particularly in Britain. Take, for instance, the cost of shipping Showco's box of tricks from Dallas to London. It weighs 20,000 lbs. and at a freight cost of 68¢ per pound, that works out at $13,608. Add to that handling charges, trucking from base to airport and vice-versa, crew's fare, insurance and so on, and there is no change left from $16,000. A large scale British hall, like Hammersmith Odeon, holds about 4000 people, so at an average of $2.00 per seat it will take more than two nights simply to pay for this one item.

In the case of Wings, the British tour is part of a much larger plan, including trips to Australia, Europe and the United States. For many groups, however, even without the expense of bringing over American equipment, the cost of a tour is beyond their resources. In such cases it is usually borne by their record company, who lay out the money in expectation of increased album sales as a result of live appearances. 'Support groups' who play the first half

of many shows may even have to pay for the privilege. They reckon it is worth it for the exposure to a large audience, although the advantage of a support position is debatable.

Bodyguard

Apart from his super-fit appearance, nothing about Brian Hunt conforms to the popular conception of a bodyguard; no scars, no broken nose, no ominous bulge beneath the left armpit. A quiet, friendly man, he describes his job as 'striking a balance'.

He waits at the side of the stage while the show is on, his eyes on the area immediately in front. If over-enthusiastic fans try to climb up, Brian's job is to stop them—"but as gently as possible," he emphasizes. He follows McCartney and the band back to the dressing-rooms and then out to the waiting cars. This is the most difficult part, the moment when striking a balance is important.

"Somebody like Paul really *likes* to see his fans, say 'hello', sign autographs and all that. But there's so many round the stage door that, with the best will in the world, things can get out of hand. I have to sum up the situation and make sure that he doesn't get mobbed, but never be heavy-handed about it."

Brian is amazingly skillful in this kind of situation, always smiling and apparently enjoying the fun, but always in exactly the right place.

"Hold on a minute, love," he says to an excited girl fan who is shoving her way to the front. "Give us a bit of room to breathe." Gentle, matey, but utterly immovable, he seems to stroll along beside the McCartneys as they head for their car.

The following morning, as the Wings party come down to breakfast looking a bit bleary-eyed, Brian is sitting in the hotel lobby reading the morning paper.

"Taking it easy this morning," he grins. "Just a couple of miles gentle run and a few push-ups before breakfast. Nothing too strenuous."

Management

Because of the enormous, world-wide scale of their operations, Wings need an efficient and high-powered business organization to hold everything together. This takes the form of McCartney Productions Limited and associated companies which operate from an office in the West End of London. At the head is Brian Brolly, a man of vast experience in this side of pop music.

Everyone has heard grisly stories of pop stars whose lives and work are not their own, of managers and agents who grow rich while the artist himself sinks deeper and deeper into the morass of debt and dependence. The whole aim of McCartney Productions, as Brian Brolly explains, is to prevent this state of affairs.

"Paul owns the company and our role is to provide a secure basis for him to work. He can compose, record, make concert tours with Wings and generally concentrate on his creative life in the firm knowledge that the benefits will accrue to him and the other members of the band. What all of us do—managers, lawyers, financial and business experts of all kinds—reflects their needs. And we aim to produce a structure which does this honestly, morally and with integrity."

In short, it is the opposite of the 'fast buck' mentality. Brolly believes in long-term strategy. The British tour, for example, and the trip to Australia which follows it, are not in themselves money-spinners. But they enable fans in these countries to see the band and reinforce the success of the records. A subsequent American tour will, of course, be profitable and an impatient, grasping management would have gone for it first. But a slow build-up, apart from giving pleasure to thousands, establishes Wings as a performing band. It gives them confidence and

Management team Alan Crowder and Brian Brolly with two roadies

27

perfects their presentation.

Working alongside Brian Brolly is Alan Crowder, an expert in the international copyright and recording field. He takes care of every administrative stage in the making of a Wings record. When it has been made he ensures that it is released at the right time, marketed effectively and promoted hard. He also keeps an eye on the sales figures that come in from all over the world, and travels with Wings wherever they go.

There are few strict job definitions in the rock world. "When I joined McCartney Productions I asked Brian Brolly what I should call myself. He said 'Oh . . . what about Management Executive?' So that's what I am. Basically, if you pick up the phone, you deal with the problem—whatever it may be."

The Touring Bus

The crew leave each town at 8:00 A.M., but the band get under way at a more comfortable hour, usually about noon. Everyone travels in the coach, although two Rolls Royce limousines accompany it in convoy. They are needed mainly to transfer McCartney and Wings from hotel to theater and back.

The bus itself looks quite ordinary from the outside, but the interior is more like a first-class railway carriage. There is plenty of space between the seats and some are arranged facing each other with tables between. At the rear is a toilet cubicle, a kind of mini-kitchen with shelves of canned food, bread and vegetables, and a small refrigerator which runs off its own generator.

On the first morning of the tour a very

ordinary, rather bedraggled vehicle arrived to pick up the band. As soon as they arrived in Southampton, Brian Brolly dismissed it and demanded the luxury bus he had ordered. When this arrived it had no refrigerator and one had to be installed overnight. This may sound like a needless fuss, but, as Brolly points out, the band are going to have to spend whole days aboard the bus for a couple of weeks, and what might be alright for a quick trip to Blackpool is intolerable if you've got to be relaxed and ready to give a show at the end of each journey.

It is a curious sensation to be stuck in a traffic jam aboard this wondrous machine. All around are cars and buses with faces turned in disbelief, watching the inhabitants preparing snacks, passing drinks around and generally carrying on as though in a long, thin kitchen-diner. The McCartneys tend to sit in aisle seats, away from the window, but the bus itself is a celebrity on its own account.

Because they travel as a family, the McCartneys have with them some people whom you would not normally find on a rock tour, including a nurse for the two younger children and a tutor for Heather. There's no escape from education, even travelling with a superstar.

Fun Club

Some groups have official fan clubs which they run as ·a kind of business offshoot. The Wings Fun Club (yes *Fun*, not Fan)· is small by comparison, but it has a friendliness and sincerity which the giant operations cannot match.

Sue, the Secretary, orginally ran the club from her South London home, keeping her files and stock of fan material in the garage. The club now has a London office but Sue still deals with everything personally, although the Wings management give her a hand with the administration.

There are about 7000 members, half of them in the United States. All it needs to join the Fun Club is a letter to Sue enclosing the entrance fee. Club members receive a membership package, a

newsletter (really a small illustrated magazine), and occasional surprise items. They can also buy specially-made tee shirts, posters, pictures etc.

The tone of the newsletter is refreshingly unpatronizing. Instead of the mindless drivel about ' favorite food', ' favorite colour', 'sign of the zodiac', which these publications often contain, it has informative articles about real events, interviews, news of current Wings activities and some exclusive photographs. The Fun Club also gets invitations to special functions, like the private performance before this tour, and television shows, and reserves a number of seats at concerts especially for members.

Sue finds out what kind of things the Wings fans want from letters which reach her from all over the world. "Anything fans send, to Capitol records or Apple or anywhere else, seems to find its way to me in the end."

20-year-old Andrew Boddington is a founder-member of the Fun Club. A Beatles fan since the age of eight, he transferred his allegiance to Paul McCartney when the group broke up. He kept the McCartney banner flying at school in the face of strong counter attacks from a heavy brigade of Led Zeppelin and Black Sabbath fans, and owns every album and single that Paul McCartney has made.

It was a great moment for him when he was awarded one of the much sought-after tickets to Wings' pre-tour final rehearsal.

Andrew has very clear preferences in the McCartney repertoire, and thinks that the finest song of all is 'Maybe I'm Amazed' from the first solo album, with 'Love In Song' and 'Jet' coming very close.

Superfan Andrew Boddington

Recording

"When I was a kid I didn't have much money—not enough to chuck about anyway—but most Saturdays I'd got enough saved to go down and buy a record. It was like the high-spot of the week, that record—I couldn't wait to get home and play it.

"So now when we're making records I always put myself back into the same position, back to those Saturday mornings in the record shop, and try to remember the things I liked. Apart from the music, a record was a nice thing to have—or it could be if it had good pictures and some notes on the sleeve, and didn't look cheap and tatty.

"And no cheating, because I've been cheated myself a few times. Like when I found this Little Richard album that I'd never seen before. When I played it I found there were only two tracks by Little Richard; the rest was by Buck Ram and his Orchestra. You need a magnifying glass to find that out from the sleeve!

"It's rotten, that kind of thing. We always try and do the opposite, give something extra with a record."

Studio 2 at EMI's recording complex in Abbey Road, North London, is authentic holy ground. Here the Beatles recorded all their hits, including the history-making 'Sergeant Pepper', and their most striking album cover shows them marching over the zebra crossing opposite the studio entrance.

But to the unenchanted eye Studio 2 looks a rather dismal place, more like a warehouse than a shrine. Its generally bedraggled air is not improved by the tarnished paintwork which, so the story goes, EMI are reluctant to freshen up for fear of affecting the room's marvellous acoustics.

All recording studios are arranged to the same overall pattern. There is the studio itself, where the artists play and sing, and a control room, separated from it by a soundproof, double-glazed window. Here the producer and the engineers go through the fearsomely compli-

cated process of collecting the music on tape. Twenty years ago this would have been quite a simple operation. After a few preliminary adjustments the group would perform its number, half a dozen microphones would carry the sound to the tape machine, and that would be it. But the pace of innovation has been breathtaking and is still gathering momentum. Today the sound that an artist puts into a microphone is only the start, the raw material, of a creative process with limitless possibilities.

The sophisticated electronics which make this possible are contained in the two main components of the control room: the mixing console, which gathers and balances the sounds, and the tape machine which stores them. A typical modern console, like the EMI-Neve desk, can take 24 microphone signals simultaneously and vary the strength and character of each one in relation to the others. So when Joe English sits at his drum kit and plays a simple rock pattern, each drum and cymbal has its own microphone—eight in all—and Tony Clarke, the engineer, can adjust them all to get the effect he wants.

All these 24 inputs can then be fed through the tape machine, which will record each of them on a separate horizontal segment or 'track' of the tape. This means that the tape itself has to be two inches wide.

This equipment is normally handled by a two-man team: the engineer, who sits at the console, and his junior partner the tape operator, who handles the recording machine. Most tape operators are on the way to becoming engineers themselves. Mark Vigars, Tony Clarke's assistant at the Wings session, is already taking charge of sessions in his own right and will soon pass over all tape operating to a newcomer. This is the normal pattern and it seems to work well. A would-be engineer usually starts as an errand boy and odd-job man and, given luck and talent, works his way up.

Top engineers like Glynn Johns (the Rolling Stones' man) or Geoff Emerick find themselves in enormous demand, with schedules that take

Recording engineer, Tony Clarke

them all over the world. Emerick first worked with Paul McCartney on the Beatles albums, assisting George Martin. But it was the Wings album, 'Band On The Run', that put Emerick into the international class, particularly since he received a 'Grammy' award (the record equivalent of an Oscar) for his work on that record.

All the time Wings are working on a song in the studio, Tony Clarke is trying out possible combinations of sound. The four huge high-quality speakers mounted above the console give out an ever-changing pattern as he works on the switches and faders. Sometimes everything vanishes except for the deep thud of the bass drum, then the whole band will burst through, to be replaced by Denny Laine's voice alone, singing a harmony part. It is necessary to be absolutely sure that each individual element is clear and sharp at this stage, so that all the colours of the palette will be available on the tape for the final mix.

The band look very different from the way they appear on stage. Each member is fenced in by movable acoustic screens to achieve 'separation', and Joe English is entirely encased in a double-glazed booth, rather like a telephone box. The sound of one instrument or voice must not spill over into anyone else's microphone, or Tony Clarke will be unable to disentangle them later. This arrangement makes it very difficult for Wings to hear each other, so they normally wear headphones (known as 'cans' in the trade) to feed the whole effect to them.

The concentration is intense and, as at rehearsals, it is sometimes broken by moments of relaxing lunacy. McCartney suddenly goes into an operatic send-up of 'My Love' which is greeted through the control room microphone by ribald cries of, "Send 'im off, Ref! Send 'im to the Eurovision Song Contest!" McCartney bows. "Thank you, music lovers everywhere!"

When the song has been performed to every-

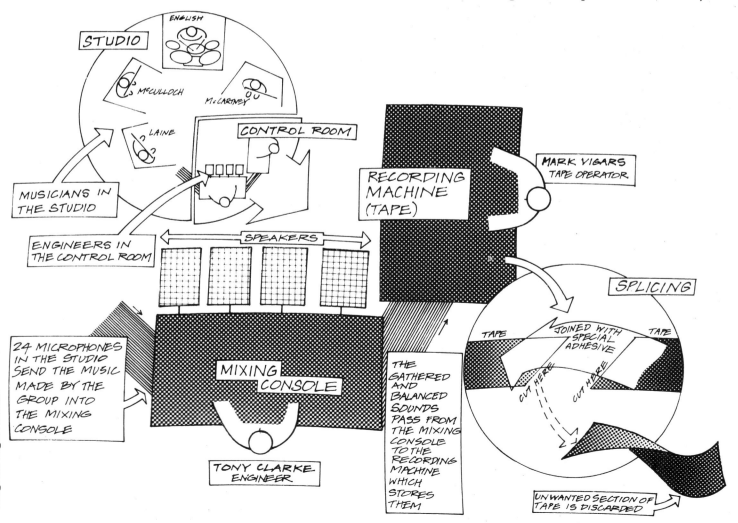

Diagram Nigel Holmes

one's satisfaction the most delicate process begins. The tape contains everything that has been done, plus, perhaps, additional parts added to the original performance and recorded on blank tracks. The task now is to 'mix' the recording into a final form.

The 24 tracks have to be mixed in the right proportions and reduced to the two tracks of a stereo record, hence the word 'reduction' which applies to this process. It takes a very acute ear and a great deal of experience to achieve a good reduction and produce a stereo 'picture'. Should the lead voice be 'in front' or should it be merged into the overall sound? Are the drums to be to the right, left or centre? A lot of trial and error can go into this until an acceptable sound is achieved. Echo and other spatial effects can be added and bits from different versions spliced in to create a perfect performance.

To see an expert engineer cutting and splicing a tape is fascinating. He runs it at normal speed up to the point at which he wants to cut and then slowly rocks it backwards and forwards over the playing head, making extraordinary whooshing noises. He can recognize each musical sound in this weird groaning. Having located the exact place, he lifts the tape out of the machine, cuts it diagonally with a blade and pulls away the unwanted section. Then he cuts and joins it again with a special adhesive. Since the tape normally passes the head at 15 inches (38 cms) per second he can place this cut at a microscopic instant in time.

Producers

In most cases the whole process, from recording to final mix, is in the hands of a producer. Originally producers were employees of the record company with absolute power over an artist's sound. This is where the myths come from—tales of electronic Svengalis who can turn 98 pound weaklings into potent super heroes, and turn them back again at will. It was never quite like that, but in the early days of the Beatles, for instance, the musicians simply hadn't the technical knowledge to do anything but observe what the producer did to turn out the

recorded sound. George Martin was the Beatles' man and they learned from him. Nowadays McCartney, drawing from his long experience, does his own production, in conjunction with the engineer.

Elton John, on the other hand, works closely with his producer, Gus Dudgeon. The two men have built up such mutual trust and understanding that they think as one in the studio. This kind of relationship often develops between artist and producer, as in the case of Yes and Eddie Offord, or, in another musical idiom, between the late Otis Redding and Steve Cropper.

Sometimes the production can swamp the personality of the artist so that, however great the sound may be, it seems anonymous. Phil Spector's 'River Deep Mountain High' is a classic of pop music and a milestone in production history, but it is his record rather than Ike and Tina Turner's, who were, after all, the artists with their names on the label. Now that Ike produces their records himself, the distinctive power of the Turners is clearly conveyed.

To produce oneself is a risky undertaking because, as producer Mickie Most remarked, it's difficult to stand aside from your own work as a performer and see its faults clearly. It takes nerve and judgment.

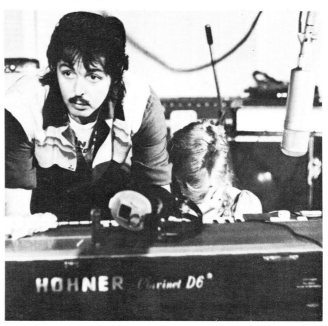

Manufacturing Records

Now comes the crucial stage at which the whole thing is turned from invisible magnetic patterns on the master tape into the familiar grooves of a plastic disc.

The transfer engineer has a high-precision lathe on which he mounts a blank disc, called a 'laquer'. As he plays the tape, the lathe's heated needle cuts a continuous spiral groove with tiny variations of depth and thickness. He

Making a Stamper

The finished Stamper

Checking the finished Record

Sleeving Records

checks that everything is working properly by watching the tip of the needle through a microscope. The cutting must be perfect because all subsequent discs, including the one you buy in the shop, will be an exact copy of this laquer.

When he is satisfied, the transfer engineer sends the laquer to the factory—in Wings' case, the vast EMI plant at Hayes, Middlesex. Here it is covered with silver nitrate and a nickel coating is deposited on top of that. When this coating is peeled off it has a perfect 'negative'

Pressing records

Gold disc

impression (bumps in place of grooves). This is the master disc. From this a 'mother' (positive) is made by a similar process and this, in turn, is used to make a negative 'stamper'.

The stamper is mounted on a huge hydraulic press which, coming down with a pressure of 6.6 kg. per square centimeter (approx. 100 lb. per sq. inch), turns lumps of hot black plastic into records—every microscopic detail faithfully retained from the laquer and the most subtle variation of sound clearly audible on good play-

ing equipment. There are dozens of presses, working automatically, and each one is regularly visited by one of the quality-control staff, who takes a sample, examines it and often plays it as well.

The girls in the playing-room may seem to have the ultimate fun job—sitting round and playing records. But they are highly trained to listen for what *shouldn't* be there—clicks, pops, wows, hisses—and have learned to listen *through* the music rather than *to* it. They insist

'Listeners' in the playing-room

that it hasn't spoiled their enjoyment of records at home. They listen differently, just as bank-clerks learn to look at huge sums of money simply as bits of paper while they're at work.

From the moment it comes off the press, a record is only handled with cotton gloves, to keep its surface clean. Some jobs have to be done manually or semi-manually. 'Sleeving' is one such operation. The record is slipped into its inner bag and then put into its jacket with the aid of a machine, but it is inserted carefully into the machine by hand.

Next door to the factory is EMI's distribution center The ground floor is entirely taken up by rows of shelves, containing all the records in the catalogue. A constant stream of trolleys moves slowly along, to be loaded according to the order-forms they carry. From here sealed bags of albums and singles go by van to the main London railway stations. They are put onto the special trains that carry morning newspapers to every corner of the country, and are collected at the other end by news-trucks. This arrangement ensures that records can reach the shops as quickly as your paper gets to your front door. The only delay is in delivering to offshore islands, when weather may hold up the mail-boats.

Orders from shops come in by telephone. The staff who take them also act as salespeople, telling dealers about new releases and keeping them up to date with fast-moving chart positions. At night a battery of answering-machines stands ready to deal with the demand.

Wings were awarded a gold disc for 'Venus And Mars' a month or so after it was released. Contrary to popular belief, these trophies are not made out of solid gold; they are gold-plated 'mothers'. EMI have a small gold-plating plant at the factory, in which gold, dissolved in a cyanide-tank, is deposited on the disc by having an electric current passed through it.

McCartney maintains that one of his gold discs from the Beatles era was actually a record by somebody else with a Beatles label stuck on it. But nowadays the presentation copies are always the right ones.

Silver, gold and platinum discs are awarded for numbers of copies sold, in the case of singles; for albums the criterion is the amount of money earned. It works like this:

Singles
Silver	250,000 copies
Gold	500,000 ,,
Platinum	1,000,000 ,,

Albums
Silver	$120,000
Gold	$240,000
Platinum	$400,000

No one can get a plated disc without having achieved this. "People often come and ask us to make a gold disc for them—companies wanting a special gift for their chairman or wives looking for a surprise present for their husbands—but we always refuse," says Commercial Manager Mr. G. Webb. "It would devalue the whole thing and be unfair to the artists who really earn an award."

A record jacket is more than simply an envelope to protect the disc from damage. Some critics have claimed that the jacket design is the twentieth century's chief contribution to functional art, along with advertising posters and neon signs. As the designs have become more elaborate, incorporating extra sheets, booklets and pop-up figures, the packaging has become part of the listening experience. As the record plays you look at the pictures, puzzle out the meaning of an intriguing pattern, wonder how an effect has been achieved. A good jacket will reflect the content and mood of the music, and it is all part of the 'something extra' which McCartney insists on providing with his albums.

Large record companies have their own design departments, but many groups prefer to work with independent studios specializing in this area. One of the leading teams is Hipgnosis, who produced the 'Venus And Mars' package, and the lengths to which they are prepared to go in achieving the perfect sleeve are almost inexhaustible. When Paul and Linda McCartney had the idea for 'Venus And Mars' they envisaged a centerfold of Wings standing in a lunar landscape. Po, one of the Hipgnosis partnership, flew to Los Angeles to discuss the plan with them and then began searching for a suitable location. They settled on the desert area of North California and shot dozens of pictures of the group surrounded by rocks and sand. They then built up the presentation around this, developing the theme of the two planets—red and yellow spheres—against a black, outer-space background. The theme of the album was carried through, not only into advertising material but also into the lighting of Wings' stage-show and the band's costumes.

Not all albums are as elaborately produced as this, of course. Some covers feature simple everyday objects—a tube of toothpaste or an egg—photographed from an intriguing and original angle. But no pop artist nowadays is indifferent to the packing in which his record is contained.

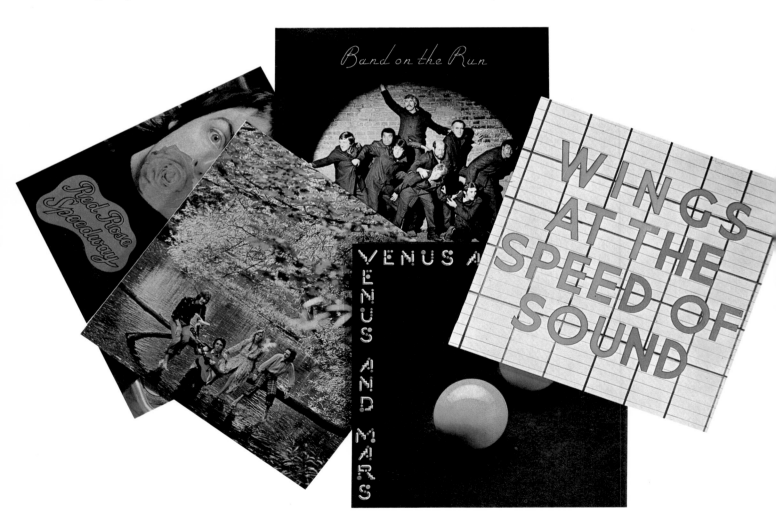

Wings' publicist Tony Brainsby

Publicity

Wings' publicist is Tony Brainsby. He has about a dozen regular clients and also looks after visiting stars while they are in Britain. His main concern is to supply the media with stories and pictures, arrange interviews and find the right kind of exposure for his artists.

Because of McCartney's eminent position there is no problem in getting publicity. The members of Wings can get on with their private lives without having to be in constant attendance at eye-catching events. When he is not touring McCartney is a very retiring man, preferring the bosom of his family to bright lights and big occasions.

When looking at a potential client, Tony Brainsby seeks out the personal characteristics which might catch the public imagination. "It's no good trying to *create* an image," he says. "No one can act a part 24 hours a day. I simply try to

focus on what is there already. You can always tell when someone has the potential to be a star. There's a quality about their personality that hits you straight away. Once that's been established it's just a matter of keeping the ball rolling."

"To be successful," he observes, "an artist must have four effective people behind him: his manager, agent, publicist and recording-manager. If any one of these doesn't do a good job the whole effort will collapse. I've seen many talented artists fall by the wayside because their manager made the wrong decision or the record company failed to push at the right moment."

Rock music is reported and discussed widely in the press. There are three major British weeklies devoted to the subject—'Melody Maker', 'New Musical Express' and 'Sounds'—as well as the international fortnightly, 'Rolling Stone', several teenage journals and a number of other

The McCartneys with Chris Welch of Melody Maker

specialist magazines such as 'Black Music', which deals exclusively with soul and reggae. In addition, many daily and Sunday papers carry columns of concert and record reviews.

The writers depend very much on people like Tony Brainsby to keep them informed in advance of events which their readers will want to hear about. He sends out concert tickets and arranges for copies of new records to be delivered.

It is difficult to say how much effect the press has on a rock artist's career. The specialist papers can certainly raise the temperature by rave notices, a classic example being the huge boost they gave to Bruce Springsteen in late 1975. Daily papers tend to concentrate on 'newsy' items, usually to do with a star's private life, his income or his brushes with authority.

Oddly enough, McCartney did not have a notably good press until about two years ago. One rock weekly in particular, took a somewhat distainful attitude. ("Ol' Doe-Eyes Is Back," said a NME headline.) This is probably because he makes no bones about being an entertainer, a position which the 'rock culture' finds naive. He makes light of it, but it hurts him nevertheless. McCartney's following is so enormous and devoted, however, that press carping is only a minor annoyance.

Selling

The one essential ingredient in the making of a hit single is radio exposure which, in Britain, means BBC Radio One. The biggest radio audience is reached during the day by disc jockeys like Noel Edmonds, Tony Blackburn and Johnny Walker, and to get to Number One a record has to be played on their shows.

Oddly enough, the DJs themselves have nothing to do with choosing the potential hit records. There is a weekly list of 56 records which is decided by the producers of the four main daily shows, and this 'playlist' goes for everybody—plus the occasional 'Golden Oldie', request and a separate 'new release' list.

How is the playlist made up? The British Market Research Bureau takes a sample of sales from secretly-selected dealers and they are delivered to Broadcasting House every Tuesday morning. The producers then sit down and decide on how much to play of what. If a record is going up it gets more plays; coming down it gets less. It's rather like the chicken and the egg: to be successful you must be on the playlist —to be on the playlist you must be successful.

The way onto the ladder is via the 'new release' spot, and here an established star like Paul McCartney is in a strong position.

Once a record has appeared in the charts, even at the bottom, there is a great jump in sales, because dealers wait for this moment before ordering their stocks. A dealer can't possibly order every record that comes out, and if he just trusts to luck and his personal taste he could be left with an expensive pile of scrap plastic by the end of the month. So he waits for the charts. The most important thing now is to have enough records to send to the shops. Alan Crowder watches the situation keenly, ready to make all kinds of fuss if the supply looks like drying up.

"If a record is moving faster than ours, they may stop pressing ours for a bit to catch up with orders for the other one. After all, there's only a limited number of presses at the factory. But you mustn't run out of stock, not even for a day. People are impatient; they set out to buy a particular record, but if they can't get it they'll go on to their second choice."

The U.K. sales-figures are sent to him daily, while those from around the world come in at monthly intervals. At the office complicated charts and graphs are drawn up to help plan future releases.

EMI sales-representative Terry Breen's round brings him twice-a-month to Chris Wellard's Record Shop in Eltham, South-East London. The first of these visits he devotes to taking orders for the new releases, while the second takes care of special campaigns, extra issues and general promotion.

A shop of average size, like this one, will probably order 25 initial copies of a new album by a major group, together with a selection of earlier 'back catalogue' items to meet the renewed demand stimulated by the promotional campaign.

Record-store windows represent a very valuable advertising medium for the companies and EMI, like all the others, are eager to take advantage of the fact. Window displays are becoming more and more sophisticated—almost small works of art in their own right—and material for this purpose is always on hand. EMI even have their own team which travels round setting up window and counter displays. When a touring band like Wings comes to town, most local shops will feature one of these elaborate shows and, while it is difficult to measure exactly the impact that they have on sales, Terry Breen thinks it is quite considerable.

A representative spends most of his time promoting albums, since singles depend mainly on radio-play for their exposure. Chris Wellard keeps a stock of Top 50 singles, plus perennial items—party tunes and old favorites —which sell steadily over a long period. Other singles have to be ordered specially, and there are enormous numbers of them. It is a little-known fact that all the Beatles singles, from 'Love Me Do'

onwards, are still in the catalogue and can be obtained at a few days' notice, as can the whole of McCartney's recorded work.

Auditions

Groups as big as Wings usually recruit musicians whose work they know well already, but occasionally they will hold auditions if there is no one immediately available. When McCartney was looking for a drummer, after the departure of Denny Siwell, he decided to invite aspiring players to audition for the job. Like all his enterprises, this was conducted to a mammoth but carefully thought-out plan. McCartney let it be known that he was looking for someone and before long the news was all over the musical press. To aid recruitment a number of advertisements were placed in national newspapers and magazines.

Wings rented a London theatre and invited the fifty most likely-sounding applicants out of hundreds to come along and play. There were drummers from other rock groups, from cruise liners, night clubs—any place where live rock music is played. So that McCartney could listen with undivided attention, he even hired a band to play with them, while he sat in the audience.

The fifty were reduced to twenty, and then to four. Now Wings took over and played with them, giving each drummer a couple of hours— time to settle down. At the end of it all they had a drummer.

"He was a very good player," says McCartney, "but he still wasn't really what we wanted." So, after a short while, they parted company.

"I don't think auditions are much use. We won't do it again. We'll just look around quietly —go and see people playing with different bands. But it was quite an experience. Fifty different drummers playing 'Caravan'!" ('Caravan' is an old jazz standard which drummers use as a showing-off piece.)

Does he look for anything particular in a musician? "Not any special style, in fact the opposite. We look for someone who can play *all* styles, because the music is so varied. The important thing is understanding, willingness, a personality that fits in."

Joe English

44

Scram-bled egg, How

Songwriting

A rock group which contains Paul McCartney is like a garage with an oil-well in the backyard—an inexhaustible supply of raw material ready to hand. In 'Rock File 3', published in 1975, author Charlie Gillett noted that McCartney had put his name to 53 hit songs, more than any songwriter since the advent of rock 'n' roll. It is an extraordinarily fertile imagination, rivalled only by John Lennon, Goffin and King, and Motown's Brian Holland. You might think that this prolific output is the result of a hard and fast system, but McCartney denies this.

"The best way to write a song is for it to write itself," he says. "Some of the best things I've done have happened like that. They turn up like magic. 'Yesterday' was one of those; I fell out of bed one morning and there was this tune. In fact it was so clear that I thought it was something I'd heard in the past, sort of lodged in the subconscious and popped out all of a sudden. But it wasn't. The tune came just like that, although I didn't have words for it. It was breakfast time so I sang, 'Scrambled egg, How I love to eat a scrambled egg . . .' until, several days later, I fitted 'Yesterday' to the first three notes and I was away.

"Most of my writing is done during periods when we're not busy working. After a few days I get the feeling I want to be doing something musical, so I go and play the piano or guitar for pleasure. It's generally at moments like this that an idea will occur to me—almost as though it's been waiting to come out."

ve to eat a   scram-bled egg.

McCartney believes that anyone can make up a song. "It may not be much good—you might have to write a hundred or so before you get into the swing of it—but there's no mystery involved. Plenty of people that don't know anything about music can do it. So long as you've got some sort of ear for music you can put a tune together."

The thing that's needed is a stimulus, a word or musical phrase to get the thing going. "When we first started writing songs everything was a nick—now there's a tip for budding songwriters! —we pinched ideas from records all the time. There's nothing immoral or dishonest about it because the imitation's only a way of getting started. Like, you might hear 'Please Mr. Postman' by the Marvelettes and be knocked out by it and want to do something in that style. So you could start off with a line like, 'Sorry Mr. Milkman . . .' By the time the song's finished you've probably got rid of that first line anyway—maybe it doesn't sound even remotely like the Marvelettes either—but it's got you going, acted as the spark. For example, in my mind 'Hey Jude' is a nick from the Drifters. It doesn't *sound* like them or anything, but I know that the verse, with those two chords repeating over and over, came when I was fooling around playing 'Save The Last Dance For Me' on the guitar."

McCartney doesn't write his songs on paper, although nowadays he works with a tape recorder. "I never used to use one; they were too big and clumsy to lug around. I always carried a song in my head, and I still think that's the best way. After all, if *I* can't remember the thing from one day to another, it isn't likely to be a very memorable song, is it?"

When he takes a new piece along to a Wings rehearsal McCartney often finds that it evolves quite differently from the way he envisaged it. One of the others may suggest a different tempo, or perhaps the very process of playing through a tune will bring out some unexpected aspect of it. Developing the final form of a song is a co-operative effort, particularly when the group contains people like Denny Laine and Jimmy McCulloch who are talented writers themselves and also contribute material to the repertoire.

The creation of a song is a mysterious process and no one has ever been able to explain satisfactorily how it happens. Paul McCartney certainly can't account for it, although he remembers clearly the circumstances in which each of his songs has begun.

"There's no system," he says firmly. "In fact, if you find yourself getting into a routine, scrap it quick before it turns into a rut."

Glossary of Pop Music Terms

Backdrop	*Scenery etc. behind band on stage.*
Sleeving	*Putting records in their covers.*
Bootleg	*Unauthorized recording sold to the public.*
Cans	*Headphones.*
Control Boards	*Portable equipment, mounted on boards, to control P.A. (qv) and lighting (qv).*
Control Room	*Part of recording studio where sound is mixed etc., and where all processes other than actual performance take place.*
Dolby	*Electronic device for eliminating natural 'hiss' of recording tape.*
Faders	*Sliding levers on mixing console controlling volume, bass, treble, etc.*
Feedback	*High-pitched note produced by loudspeaker when microphone or pickup (qv) is too close to it.*
Final Mix	*Reduction (qv) of many tracks to the two tracks of a stereo record.*
Fuzz Box	*Foot-operated electronic gadget which distorts the sound fed into it.*
Gig	*Slang word for a concert—large or small.*
Groupie	*Group's camp-follower, usually female, often encountered by Sunday newspaper reporters but rarely by anyone else.*
Horns	*All wind instruments.*
Laquer	*Record cut directly, not pressed.*
Leslie	*Brand-name of organ speaker much favored by rock bands.*
Lighting gantry	*Framework, usually scaffolding, to hold lights.*
Mellotron	*Electronic instrument capable of reproducing the sounds of other instruments by the use of pre-recorded.tape.*
Mixing Console	*Control gear for combining signals from many sources and balancing them.*

Monitors	*Loudspeakers on stage to relay sound to band.*
Moog	*Proprietary name of popular synthesizer.*
P.A.	*Public Address System. Main speakers.*
Pickup	*Small microphone located beneath guitar strings.*
Playback	*Replay of recorded tape.*
Playlist	*List of records drawn up by producers for disc-jockeys to play.*
Plectrum	*Small implement for plucking guitar strings.*
Promo Man	*Promoter employed by recording or publishing company to get records played on the radio.*
Reduction	*Process whereby original number of tracks are mixed down to stereo balance.*
Reverb	*Lit. 'Reverberation'—electronic echo effect.*
Riff	*Repeated musical phrase.*
Rigging	*Setting up band's equipment on stage.*
Roadies	*All supporting workers travelling with group.*
Rostrum	*Platform constructed on stage.*
Runner	*Crew-member available to run messages and bring spares, food etc.*
Separation	*Differentiation of individual voices and instruments.*
Stack	*Complete assemblage of speakers.*
Stamper	*Die used in pressing copies of record.*
Track	*Segment of recording tape carrying an individual instrument or voice.*
Wah Wah Pedal	*Foot-operated device for changing tonal characteristics of a note. Gives a sound like 'wah-wah'.*

MIDLAND HOTEL.

PAUL McCARTNEY & WINGS ROOMING LIST
****

BAND	Room No.	CREW BAND	Room No.
Paul & Linda McCartney - 1 dbl. suite	221/9	Trevor Jones - twin John Hammill	216
McCartney children (three) 1 triple	237	Peter Morley Thomas Sellen - twin	218
Rose Martin single ******************	247	Derek Unwin - Twin Andy Collins	222
Gary Foskett single	257	Ray Watouski Ian Peacock - twin	230
Mr. & Mrs. Laine double	240	Craig Schertz Maurice Lyda - twin	156
Mr. & Mrs. Dorsey Double and child & extra bd.	351/3.	Kirby Wyatt Alan Owen - twin	160
Jimmy McCulloch single	215	Jack Maxson - single	164/162
Joe English Single	238	Pamela Keats - single	242
Stephen Howard single	149	Steve Mately - single	130
Thaddeus Richard single	263	Ian Knight - single	132
Howie Casey single	209	Coach driver - single	274
Brian Brolly single	273	Truck driver Truck driver - twin	152
Alan Crowder single	275	Clint Jones - single	224.
Barry Humphries single	277		
Bob Ellis single	226		
Tony Brainsbury single	168		
Brian Hunt single	158		
Ann Bush single	146		
Steve Coton single	136		
Patrick Barthropp Co. single (chauffeurs) " "	120		
" " single	126		
Coach driver single ******************	281		
Ann Gillham single	268.		

M. BUSH. 241

GEE WIZARD SINGLE 249

GEE WIZARD TWIN 261.

**The Publishers wish to thank
McCartney Productions Limited for their
co-operation in producing this book.**